I'm convinced that our people will be generous if they believe the church is generous. —Tom Berlin

The Generous Church

A Guide for Pastors

TOM BERLIN

From the author of *Defying Gravity*

Abingdon Press / Nashville

THE GENEROUS CHURCH
A GUIDE FOR PASTORS

Copyright © 2016 Abingdon Press
All rights reserved.

No part of this work may be reproduced or transmitted in any form or by any means, electronic or mechanical, including photocopying and recording, or by any information storage or retrieval system, except as may be expressly permitted by the 1976 Copyright Act or in writing from the publisher. Requests for permission can be addressed to Permissions, The United Methodist Publishing House, PO Box 280988, 2222 Rosa L. Parks Blvd., Nashville, TN 37228-0988 or e-mailed to permissions@umpublishing.org.

This book is printed on elemental chlorine-free paper.

Library of Congress Cataloging-in-Publication data applied for.
978-1-5018-1349-8

Scripture quotations unless noted otherwise are from the Common English Bible. Copyright © 2011 by the Common English Bible. All rights reserved. Used by permission. www.CommonEnglishBible.com.

Scripture quotations marked NRSV are taken from the New Revised Standard Version of the Bible, copyright 1989, Division of Christian Education of the National Council of the Churches of Christ in the United States of America. Used by permission. All rights reserved.

16 17 18 19 20 21 22 23 24 25 — 10 9 8 7 6 5 4 3 2 1
MANUFACTURED IN THE UNITED STATES OF AMERICA

*To the church members who made giving a way of life.
With deep thanks to those who pushed me
to have courage and to challenge the church
to fulfill Christ's calling to generosity.*

CONTENTS

Foreword 7

1. The Generous Church. 11

2. The Role of the Leader 29

3. Plan It 43

4. Communicate It. 59

5. Manage It 77

Notes 96

FOREWORD

I am convinced that people want to attend a generous church. My wife Karen and I once visited a church while on vacation. Entering a few minutes late, we found the first hymn well under way. I fumbled with the bulletin, trying to find a page number. (This was before the time when lyrics were projected on a screen.) The woman in front of us turned around, handed me her hymnal, and pointed out the verse. "So glad you are here," she whispered. Thinking back on that day, I can't remember the details of the sermon. The prayer concerns are long forgotten. The Scripture was found somewhere in the Bible, but that is all I know. What I do recall is the woman who saw our need and responded with what she had. She was generous. It was a small thing, but it made me want to be a part of her church.

The generous church is full of members like that. They show generosity in many things, including their time, compassion, talent, money, and attention to the ministry of their church. Often they did not start that way. They learned those habits by being part of a congregation that defined its life with the value of generosity.

I recently wrote a stewardship program for Abingdon Press called *Defying Gravity: Break Free from the Culture of More.* In the program, I talk about the dynamics of money and possessions in our society that make generosity difficult, and I explore ways people can discover the joy of generosity. My study of this topic has given me a deep appreciation for those who live a generous life. It has reminded me that generosity is the foundation not just for that particular program but for any stewardship program and, in fact, for the lives of all Christians.

It is apparent to me that in order for Christians to become generous, they need the teachings of Christ related to love, money, and compassion as those teachings apply to everyday life. They need the examples of other believers. They need to learn how to manage money so they will have resources to give others.

Most importantly, however, I have come to realize that Christians need the help of a church that itself is generous. When the church is focused on sharing the gospel message so that others will receive salvation, then the giving that once felt like a hardship becomes a joy. When the church blesses the poor and vulnerable and fulfills Mary's prophesy that God "has filled the hungry with good things" (Luke 1:53a), then people are excited to join the mission.

One of the most generous people I know is Janet, a woman who has given regularly over the years to the church I serve. Janet is on a fixed income. She lives in a modest apartment. She has few possessions. She often gives her time to other residents in her building who are older and have limited mobility. She will never be one of our largest financial donors, but I know that every offering she makes is a major gift when considered as a percentage of her income. Like the widow Jesus observed sharing her coins in the temple, Janet gives her best to God.

Janet's generosity is based on God's generosity. But it has another point of reference, which is Janet's belief in the church where she gives.

> The things the church does help people who need help. The outreach is good, and I trust they are doing what they say they are doing. It is nice to know it is reliable and the results you share are encouraging. The people the church helps appreciate what you are doing for them. That is what makes it so great and rewarding to the people who are volunteering as well as those who are receiving. When you give to the church, you know that your money is going to the people who need what you give.

Janet is a discerning donor. Notice that she values impact. She wants her church to use money well. She is grateful that the church communicates the outcomes of its ministry so she can be encouraged by the results. She also has trust that the money she gives is handled well and is allocated to the purposes for which it was given.

Note that, for generous people such as Janet, this combination of intentionality of ministry, demonstrated results, communication, and trust is a powerful incentive to give. These generous Christians don't just want to give to a church. They want to be a part of something bigger and do something more than they can do on their own. They want to make a difference in the world, in the name of Christ. That is why they give their time, talent, and money to churches that demonstrate generosity.

In a church setting, generosity is both a root and a fruit. As a root, it is a way of drawing resources, people, and energy into the life of a congregation. Churches that make ministry plans, set goals, and create deadlines discover that people share their resources when the church demonstrates it is ready to receive them. When the church shows itself to be generous, resources are pulled in like iron filings to a magnet.

As a fruit, generosity shows itself in many ways. It is in the culture and ministry of the congregation whose actions are consistent with the love and grace of Christ. People are attracted by plans that will bless others, by ideas that will solve problems, and by the deep desire of a church to bring God's goodness to the hardships of the world. When churches loiter in wishful thinking rather than stepping out in the adventure of sacrificial doing, they will never be the recipients of generosity.

The goal of this book is to help you consider how to become a generous church or, if the church is already generous, how to become more generous. Generosity in any form is a way of living that honors God through joy and the grace shown to others. It is reflected in the way we follow the pattern of life that Christ demonstrated in his ministry.

Many factors are at play when churches become generous. Each chapter in this book will offer a different look at the goals, values, and practices of your congregation so you can become a church where people will offer their best for the glory of God.

1

THE GENEROUS CHURCH

BUILDING A BRAND

When I was a kid, I lived next door to a friend who gave me a ride to school every morning in a Volkswagen Beetle. The Beetle, also known as the Bug, was a great car to drive. It was more than a car, having been given a fun and playful personality that was a part of the *Herbie* films that came out between 1968 and 2005. Herbie, a VW Bug, was an energetic and loyal friend in those films. My neighbor felt the same about her Bug. She gave it a name and would talk to it as she drove, encouraging and cajoling it. As odd as it may sound, she and that car had a relationship.

Over the years I knew other people who had relationships with their Volkswagens. A neighbor with free-range hair owned a VW Camper Van that had large flower stickers in the windows. It was the ultimate hippie van, a vehicle that held little communities of people who enjoyed nature and were at peace with the universe. Another friend owned a VW Rabbit. During the gas shortage of the 1980s, he would brag about how little gas his Rabbit used as he drove to school and work. Unlike the majority of drivers, who ambled around town in large gas-guzzlers before waiting in lines at the service station, his efficient and economical Rabbit was a part of the solution to the fuel shortage.

During those years, Volkswagen built a brand and attracted new generations of drivers not only in the United States but around the globe. In the 1990s, Volkswagen ads captured the essence of their brand with the word *fahrvergnügen*, which meant "driving pleasure." This German company became a leader in Europe and abroad, buying other car manufacturers and adding more brands until, by 2015, they were the number-two car company in the world.[1]

Brands are hard to create. They take time and are built through a string of consistent decisions, when product after product delivers a promised experience in new and better ways as the decades unfold. Volkswagen's brand was built on the idea that you can have a relationship with your vehicle, that driving can be fun, and that cars do not have to despoil the environment. VW drivers had special feelings about their cars and a sense of community with each other. In an odd but powerful way, the VW brand reflected their personalities and values.

WHAT'S YOUR BRAND?

Here is a question that church leaders would be wise to consider: What brand are you building in your church? Just as the VW brand has certain values that buyers identify with, your church has values that are communicated and put into practice every day. What are those values? Is generosity among them?

You may resist the idea of a church having a "brand." The word smacks of business and marketing and seems out of place in a conversation about the theology and values of a church. But the exercise is valuable as a way to think about what you are doing as a local congregation.

One way to identify a brand is to state the central values being expressed through its services or products. A church might consider verses from Jesus' teachings that sum up the life of their Christian community. It is helpful to identify verses that sum up what a particular congregation finds essential in their life together.

Imagine a group of church leaders on a retreat who decide to identify four key verses from the Gospels that will guide their ministry. The verses, once selected, will be placed across the top of the four sanctuary walls, to remind the congregation of its identity each time they gather for worship or congregational meetings. The leaders spend time reviewing the Gospels. Many verses are offered for consideration. After a great deal of discussion, the list is narrowed to the following five, and the group finds it almost impossible to delete one more:

> "All who want to save their lives will lose them. But all who lose their lives because of me and because of the good news will save them." (Mark 8:35)

"I was hungry and you gave me food to eat. I was thirsty and you gave me a drink. I was a stranger and you welcomed me. I was naked and you gave me clothes to wear. I was sick and you took care of me. I was in prison and you visited me."

(Matthew 25:35-36)

The Spirit of the Lord is upon me
because the Lord has anointed me.
He has sent me to preach good news to the poor,
to proclaim release to the prisoners
and recovery of sight to the blind,
to liberate the oppressed,
and to proclaim the year of the Lord's favor.

(Luke 4:18-19)

"I am the vine; you are the branches. If you remain in me and I in you, then you will produce much fruit." (John 15:5a)

"Therefore, go and make disciples of all nations, baptizing them in the name of the Father and of the Son and of the Holy Spirit, teaching them to obey everything that I've commanded you. Look, I myself will be with you every day until the end of this present age." (Matthew 28:19-20)

Looking at these and other verses that were set aside, it occurs to one church member that the underlying quality that Jesus calls for in every aspect of Christian discipleship is generosity. God is initially generous to us, creating us. Then God shares love, forgiveness, and other forms of grace in our lives. Like branches grafted to a vine, we draw our strength and resources from God.

As the church leaders consider God's generous nature, it is hard for them to ignore another key verse that had not been listed.

"God so loved the world that he gave his only Son, so that everyone who believes in him won't perish but will have eternal life." (John 3:16)

If you were to go through a similar process in your church, the results would be a bit different, but at some point it's likely you would identify generosity as an underlying principle of Christian faith.

Through faith in Christ, we find new life and salvation. God is generous with us from our inception to the moment we are offered the Resurrection. As a result, the calling of Christ upon our lives is not arduous but a yoke that is easy and a burden that is light. Christ followers are called to be generous in return, sharing the love of Christ that now resides in their lives. They share their resources with others, caring for the sick and poor. Jesus' disciples are generous with those who have no faith in God and are willing to talk about what they believe and how Christ has transformed them.

The teaching ministry of the church is a way that believers help each other go deeper, learn the meaning of the Bible, explore doctrine, and share stories about heroes of the faith. Church members care for one another through acts of kindness and compassion. They are a light to the world in the distinct fellowship they experience, as they celebrate each other's accomplishments and bear each other's burdens.

It does not take long to realize that the Christian life is a generous life. It is generous in love, forgiveness, compassion, kindness, hospitality, healing, faith, and so many other ways. In our story above, the group of church leaders realizes that if they can demonstrate the generosity of their church ministry in these ways, many people will want to join them. Who does not want to enjoy a generous life?

Let me go out on a limb here: If I had to choose one word to describe the totality of a life directed by the Lordship of Christ, my choice would be *generous*. This is the most important issue that the church has to confront in our time, because, though *generous* may describe the underlying theology and ministry of the New Testament church, most churches today struggle to live in a way that can be described by this important word.

To put this struggle in modern terms, we are not keeping the implied promises of our brand. We have a theoretical belief but not a realized theology. If you were to poll people in your community who were not church members, how many of them would describe your church as "generous"?

In churches that honor our brand and show generosity in all they do, a wonderful cycle is set in motion. The church is generous and blesses others. People want to attend a generous church, and they become a generous part of the congregation. Generosity begets generosity.

BRAND CONSEQUENCES

People love it when the brand delivers all that it says it will. Volkswagen hit a home run when it introduced its Type EA 189 "clean diesel" engines into several models in 2009.[2] VW promised that the new technology would deliver almost zero emissions. Customers understood that by driving one of these cars, they would honor their desire to care for the environment. What amazed most drivers was that there seemed to be no tradeoffs. The cars were quick and responsive. Acceleration was outstanding. Customers were getting the best of both worlds. The quick, sporty car that VW owners had grown to love was still in place, only now with even better fuel economy and super-low emissions.

Then, in May 2014, scientists at the University of West Virginia discovered a problem with the clean diesel engines. The low-emission readings were not real. Later it was discovered that Volkswagen had installed a computer chip that produced a false reading during emission inspections. The actual emission output was from five to thirty-five times the allowed limit in the United States, depending on the model. Worldwide, eleven million cars were affected.[3]

The impact to the Volkswagen brand was immediate. Outrage moved from country to country as the scope of the deception was discovered. VW owners were shocked that the company had sold them cars with high emissions. The impact would have been bad at any car company, but at VW the scandal was more severe because of the brand the company had built. The customers, having trusted the corporation and purchased the car for its advertised environmental benefits, were being forced to violate their ecological and sustainability values every time they got in the car and started the engine. Today, after years of building a brand, VW is in danger of losing an entire generation of customers who got burned by false advertising.

If the Christian "brand" is based on generosity, then perhaps something similar is taking place in our churches. When people attend churches that are not generous, they become frustrated. Churches demonstrate a lack of generosity when:

- *friendly* means "saying hello to old friends while ignoring first-time guests or new members"
- *loving* means "offering hospitality to those who look like the majority population while being inattentive to others or sending subtle cues that they are less welcome"
- *stewardship* means "spending money on a facility or pipe organ renovation, while ministry to the poor or money spent to reach and teach children is deemed unaffordable"

- *compassion* means "caring for the patriarchs and matriarchs of the church while the needs of less influential families escape notice"

There are many ways a church can come across as lacking generosity, and these affect the most committed church members as well as those outside the church. Church members want to live out the values of generosity they have found in Christ, but when they see little evidence of Jesus' teaching, or when they conclude the church is taking care of itself rather than giving for the sake of the world, they are like the owners of the VW models with the bad computer chip: by sitting in the pew, belonging to the church, and giving to church programs, they are violating their own values.

A variety of studies over the past several years has confirmed the decline of church attendance and membership in the United States. Mainline denominations, which have an older membership base, are the most dramatically affected by this shift in church participation. Many reasons have been given to explain the decline, ranging from lack of evangelism to poor leadership to changes in the larger culture, among others. But what if the real issue is something far more fundamental? What if the church is in decline because people have observed a gap between the teaching of Christ and the life of the congregation?

It's instructive to note that while many churches are in decline, some congregations remain as pockets of vitality. These churches seem to be performing a modern miracle. While they may not experience runaway growth, they are stable and enjoy modest gains in worship attendance. While giving has fallen precipitously in other churches, these congregations are growing in the donations entrusted to their care. They are addressing important needs in their communities and are taken seriously by local nonprofits.

Other churches are noticeably aging, but these churches include a broad range of age groups, from children to millennials to older members. At the heart of the churches' vitality is their generosity, which makes them credible witnesses to individuals and families who are seeking a more generous life.

Jesus calls the church to be generous in everything it does and to give itself away so that it will find new life in Christ. But often our churches live in grudging and miserly ways, where love is a scarce commodity, forgiveness is rarely available, compassion is parsed out in trifling doses, and true community is in low supply.

When the church lacks generosity, the brand has been compromised. New people have no incentive to attend. Existing members become uncomfortable with the gap between their personal values and the church's allocation of congregational time, talent, and treasure, which seem to serve little of what Jesus said was important in life. Because of that gap, members stop giving or, worse, stop participating at all.

GENEROUS LEADERSHIP

It is not enough for the church to hold forth a grand vision of what the world should look like while passively observing what the world actually is. People are looking for great and noble institutions, whose lives are based on what they do in the world, what they offer to others. People find meaning in being part of a congregation that helps transform the lives of those who are spiritually poor, physically or emotionally vulnerable, or socially downtrodden. What people seek, what they are willing to sacrifice time and money for, what they are willing to participate in generously themselves, are churches that live out the values and teaching of the New Testament in ways that challenge the status quo of both the society in which they live and the established church where they attend.

Churches that lack generosity are often led by individuals with a scarcity mind-set. The church leaders have a long list of reasons the church cannot do more for members or for the community. It is too hard to get volunteers. There is no money in the budget. Starting a new ministry would mean harming one that currently exists. People are not attending as they once did. These leaders give an endless list of reasons for holding on tightly when the church is called to bless others generously. As a result, such churches end up on the sidelines of life.

I am reminded of former President Theodore Roosevelt's speech "Citizenship in a Republic" given at the Sorbonne in Paris on April 23, 1910. Roosevelt called on the elite of Europe to engage in the duties of citizenship rather than living insular and selfish lives. Roosevelt could have been talking about churches when he stated,

> There is but a small field of usefulness open for the men of cloistered life who shrink from contact with their fellows. Still less room is there for those who deride of slight what is done by those who actually bear the brunt of the day; nor yet for those others who always profess that they would like to take action, if only the conditions of life were not exactly what they actually are.[4]

Roosevelt impatiently called his audience, which felt sheltered and secure in the years prior to World War I, to use their gifts and abilities for the public good. The call of the Holy Spirit to the church in our time is quite similar. I can only imagine that it is all the more urgent.

Mark Miller is the pastor of Ebenezer United Methodist Church in Stafford, Virginia. Mark has experience with the desire of his members to attend a generous church.

I had just returned from a mission exploration trip to Cuba. During that trip, I encountered numerous Pastors who were leading vibrant congregations full of people devoted to Jesus. I was deeply inspired by the ways the Holy Spirit was at work in and among the Cuban people.

In one particular town, a pastor was working with volunteers to build a church. The growth of Christianity in that particular area had been quite amazing over the past couple of years, and the church leaders were working hard to create a larger worship space, expanding from a room that might hold fifty people to a space that could hold up to 250. Resources were scarce, and yet through perseverance and prayer, the new worship space was almost completed. The Pastor shared with our team that it would probably still be several months before they could use the space, because they could not afford any kind of seating. They needed about $10,000 to purchase and install enough pews. I felt God call me to help and pledged to this Cuban pastor our church would supply the necessary funds. To this day, I am a bit surprised by my bold promise, since our church was going through its own set of financial challenges, and I had no real authority to make such a promise on behalf of our congregation.

When I stood before our congregation in worship the following Sunday, I shared my observations regarding the United Methodist Church in Cuba, and the astounding ways in which the Holy Spirit was at work there. I also sheepishly acknowledged my financial pledge to this one particular

Cuban pastor, and I apologized to the congregation for making such a commitment without prior approval. I explained that we would not be doing "fund raisers" or holding a special offering to raise funds, but that if anyone in the congregation wanted to help this church in Cuba purchase pews, they could contact me.

After worship, a member approached me with tears of joy. She shared that her father had passed away several weeks earlier and she was settling his estate. She sensed that God was encouraging her to find a way to bless others as a way of honoring her father. She placed a ten thousand dollar check into my hands and asked me to make certain that these funds were used to purchase pews for the church in Cuba. Before the end of the day, I had two more conversations with individuals who also wanted to donate the entire ten thousand dollars. When I told them that funds had already been donated, they still insisted that I accept their donations and use the funds to bless the work of other United Methodist churches in Cuba.

Through that experience, I was reminded of how people want to be part of God's work in the world, and how stories of faith will often prompt generous hearts. I still refrain from impulsively pledging financial support on behalf of my congregation, but I do feel confident that if the Holy Spirit ever leads me again in that direction, I will trust and obey, with the conviction that there are generous hearts ready and waiting to join God in the good work waiting to be accomplished.

A CHANGE OF HEART

Think about what happens when the church lives the generous life that Jesus described as the kingdom of God. Such churches have a mind-set of abundance. When they do not have money, they assume it can be raised if the importance of their endeavor is properly explained. If they don't have enough volunteers, they find ways to widen the search by asking people in the community who may not even attend their church. If a member feels called to start a new ministry, they encourage the member rather than offering reasons it won't work. These churches believe that when God gives a vision, resources will follow. They are willing to endure the discomfort of the time between identifying what they need and receiving what God will offer. Like the children of Israel in the desert, they would prefer to have all the provision for the journey up front, but they are content to pick up the manna day by day, learning to trust that God will not forget their needs as they follow God's will.

Suddenly important things are at stake every week. When the church plans to build a new Habitat for Humanity house, that decision becomes a key factor in whether a family will own a home for the first time. When church leaders ask adults to organize a Vacation Bible School at a community park in a low-income area of town, they are encouraging each other to share Christ in a new way. When a team of church members travels to Africa to work in a mission hospital, those members will be using their gifts and training in a different context. When volunteers show up at the church's annual Halloween party, welcoming new families who may have driven into the parking lot for the first time and handing out information about the church, those volunteers are demonstrating a desire to include the community. When the church holds a monthly food drive for items that will be placed in the backpacks of school children to give them nourishing food over the weekend, members are actively working to fulfill the values that they hold dear.

GENEROSITY IS ESSENTIAL

The foundation of every good thing a church does is Jesus' consistent call to be generous in every way. The generous church is a place where people want to participate. Being part of such a church is exciting, because something important is always at stake. If you don't show up for worship, you may miss a glimpse of God's grace coming into the world. If you don't give, a child may go hungry. If you don't volunteer, someone may not learn about Jesus or find an affordable home.

As the church, we must do what Jesus did. We must, out of generosity, find ways to heal the spiritual, physical, economic, and social illnesses of the local community and the world community. In so doing, we will find the truth of Jesus' admonition that "those who find their lives will lose them, and those who lose their lives because of me will find them" (Matthew 10:39).

If we don't live generously, faith becomes a form of spiritual narcissism—the church's focus is only on its members and can become especially focused on members who are the most demanding and vocal about their needs and disappointments. These are the very people most likely to hold a mind-set of scarcity, believing that we must keep all we have for fear that we might lose our life as a congregation. Driven by this fear, we decide that money cannot be spent, ministry cannot be undertaken, people should not be made uncomfortable or challenged. It takes very little time to identify a congregation that doesn't live generously.

By contrast, when we are selfless and live out the gospel, the church becomes a lamp set high on a stand, bringing light to the community. When a church lives generously—caring about the hungry, housing the homeless, ministering to the sick and grieving—then even people who are not members will spread the word about its good work. Often, sadly, their praise includes a note of surprise that the congregation does not follow the grim stereotypes that people have often held about the church in recent years.

GENEROSITY GETS AROUND

Many Christians have a hard time knowing how to share their faith in Christ. In the generous church, sharing comes naturally. When people are engaged in exciting ministries, they share their experiences with people who are curious about the Christian life or those who once were part of a congregation but dropped out.

Pam, who was active in her local church, was asked to lunch by a friend after Pam described the ministry her church provided to people in the community who were homeless. Her church, working with other congregations in the area, offered a guesthouse for a week in the winter where men and women were welcomed out of the elements each night. Meals were served. Showers were made available. A comfortable place to sleep was provided. One woman who had been living in a local shelter with her two children was mentored and assisted with transitional housing until she could save enough money for a deposit on her own place.

25

During lunch, Pam began to share other aspects of her church's ministry. She told her friend about small groups where people gathered to get to know each other as they studied the Bible. They talked about the various styles of worship that were offered each Sunday and programs for children and teenagers. They discussed other ways the church was helping people in the community and in other parts of the world. Pam was able to articulate the way Christ's teaching was reflected in those ministries. Her story of the congregation's generosity in one area soon led to a discussion of the church as a whole, and she left hopeful that her friend would attend one Sunday soon. Sharing why her faith and her church were important had rarely been so easy and natural.

When people hear stories about the many forms of generosity the church displays, they are curious and interested. Suddenly evangelism isn't a theological dueling match with spiritual doubters; it is sharing an experience and a community that enriches its members' lives. For most people, it's easy to argue with beliefs, but it's hard to argue with generous love, expressed in many ways by a community of people who hold the teaching of Christ in common.

Generosity turns the church inside out. When I was in high school, our church youth group ended meetings the same way each week. We would stand in a circle facing each other. We would cross our arms and take the hands of the people standing on either side of us. We would recite a benediction. Then, at the end, we would turn so we were facing outward. The idea behind this practice was to show that first the church may look inward—seeking a deeper relationship with God, studying the Bible and its implications for our lives, caring for each other in a community of love. It was appropriate for our group to focus on its life together; after all, a good deal of the church's generous love happens inside the life of the congregation. But we are not complete until we turn our focus outward. God's love did not come only for the church; it came for the world. The church's mission is to share that love faithfully and pursue God's call out into the community.

What I have found over the years since that weekly benediction is that if the church does not have a generous love inside the life of the congregation, it will not be generous in any real way with the world outside. What has been more surprising is the discovery that if a congregation does not want to give itself to the needs of the world, it typically becomes ingrown and stunted in its love for its members as well. Generosity works in both directions. When we truly love each other, we will love the world as Jesus loved it. The love of Christ is the root of every generous inclination and action.

But generosity never happens by accident, in the life of an individual or a church. The good news is that when churches lack generosity, it is rarely out of deceit or intentional misdirection. The problem is that churches rarely think carefully about the processes leading to generosity in the lives of the congregation or the church members. That is why leadership is so important.

2

The Role of the Leader

When it comes to generosity, church leaders typically like to talk about time and talent. Asking people to volunteer or use the skills they have developed is seen as a compliment. This is why pastors are comfortable asking people to sign up for everything from teaching Sunday school to singing Christmas carols at the nursing home. What most pastors don't like to talk about is money.

Pastors understand that the church has a budget, and budgets require planning and monthly review. They don't mind going to church finance meetings, looking at spreadsheets for income and expenses, or considering future expenses that will bolster the ministry. What pastors do not like is talking with people about personal finances or giving. Recently I was in a conversation with a pastor who put it this way:

> I just don't know how to talk about money with people. And
> I am reluctant to preach about it. I am really reluctant to
> talk to individuals about their giving, even though I know it
> would be the best thing I could do for the church.

Steven Pressfield, in his book *The War of Art* (Black Irish Entertainment LLC, 2002), talks about a force that blocks the work of creative people. He calls it *the Resistance*. The Resistance is what leads people facing creative projects to do anything but apply themselves to that task. Writers are suddenly busy watching TV when they should be writing. Painters decide to go on the hunt for the perfect brush instead of placing themselves in front of an easel. Poets feel the need for a long walk instead of putting pen to paper. Most of us understand Pressfield's description of the Resistance as something present in our own lives.

In the same way, when it comes to talking about money, pastors have what I call *the Reluctance*. We are simply hesitant to bring up the topic with other people. Many pastors don't even like to talk at length about money with couples in counseling, even though financial matters are one of the top sources of conflict in marriage. The thought of preaching about the topic is alarming. The idea of asking someone in a private conversation for a donation to the church is downright terrifying.

REASONS FOR THE RELUCTANCE

There are many reasons why clergy are hesitant to talk about money:

Inexperience

Most pastors have very little personal familiarity managing money other than their own. Most live on a limited salary and carry debt accrued while completing a degree to meet their church's educational requirements for ordination. They have little disposable income. Other people know that clergy have few personal discretionary funds and therefore don't ask them for donations or invite them to serve on nonprofit boards where they would be asked to give or raise funds. As a result, they have never seen such requests modeled.

Training

Pastors, unlike directors of other nonprofits, have little formal training in how to ask for donations. They do not attend workshops or seek certifications in fund-raising. Often they think such activities have no place in the life of the church and would ruin their relationship with their congregation.

Pastoral Concern

Clergy want to avoid role confusion. They want church members to know that their pastoral care is independent of the contributions they make to the church. They fear that if they are direct about requests for money or consideration of greater stewardship by their church members, people will be upset and unwilling to come to them for other important matters.

Perception

No one wants to be seen as self-serving. Pastors' salaries are dependent on the giving of church members. Asking for money may create the appearance that they are encouraging financial stewardship for their own sake, not for the kingdom of God. They want to shepherd the flock without being accused of shearing the wool and taking it to market for sale.

Conflict Avoidance

Pastors can easily do some basic math and figure out that few people in the church tithe. National surveys indicate that most Christians give 1 or 2 percent of their income to all charitable concerns, including their church. Pastors fearfully imagine that if they call people to greater commitment, members will be angry with them or leave the church completely.[5] Any one of these factors can lead to the Reluctance that keeps pastors silent about personal finance, materialism, and the possible good that can be done through generosity.

THE POWER OF GENEROSITY

The word *generosity* may help clergy reframe the issue entirely. This is not about money. It is about helping people experience their sanctification and providing the resources necessary for the ministry of the church. Giving is a key spiritual issue that must be considered by anyone who follows Christ. Key resources for that conversation are the Bible and Christian theology, two areas in which trained, committed clergy can provide great help.

No idolatry has a stronger hold on Christians today than their relationship with money and possessions. This fact can easily be measured in the credit card debt of Americans, the way we allocate our income, and the volume of marketing that surrounds us. We live in a culture that issues a daily call to wear the newest clothes, purchase the most recent technology upgrade, and drive the biggest truck or best-looking car.

At the same time that the siren songs of merchandising tempt us, we are trying to figure out how to make ends meet. For example, one of our greatest long-term challenges is providing a home, transportation, funds for retirement, medical care, and savings for education, while managing a host of other expenses for everyday living. If we want to be generous and meet our other financial goals, we must organize and deploy our resources thoughtfully.

Here is a place where the church can provide practical and life-transforming information. But the Reluctance is telling the pastor and other church leaders to steer clear of the topic.

BE A RESOURCE

When the church is willing to talk about issues of generosity, stewardship, and finance, it becomes a resource to its members. For people who want to grow in their love and obedience to Jesus, imagine how helpful it would be to attend a seminar or series of classes at their church to help them understand how to become a steward.

Some church members are gifted in business or have employment that has created wealth. In managing their money, they have access to accountants, stockbrokers, financial managers, attorneys, and a host of others to advise them how to invest, save, shelter, and disperse their funds. Think of the good that would come if, in a similar way, pastors were the professionals willing to talk with church members about the joy of generosity and the meaning found when we invest in activities and institutions that are laboring for the kingdom of God.

To fill this crucial role, pastors must overcome the Reluctance. They must stop thinking of financial management as some dark part of life that might leave an oily stain on their ministry. Consider instead what might happen in churches if pastors were as eager as other professionals to talk about these matters. No matter what income level people occupy, if they are willing to become stewards of their funds and offer a tithe to God, they will be some of the most dependable and generous people in the church. When such people take steps to live as financial stewards, they support and indeed make possible the ministry of the church.

PUT MONEY IN THEIR POCKETS

Many people think that when a pastor talks about finances, the goal is to take money from their pockets. But in the generous church, sermons and courses about finances are designed to put money back in their pockets.

Most people with money problems do not lack income. The issue is excessive outflow and lack of planning. Without a budget, they have no real idea how their money is spent each month. A lack of financial goals means that the world takes them by surprise month after month. The ensuing chaos in their personal finances leads to conflict in relationships and disappointment from those dependent upon them. Clearly, one area where the church can help is by teaching about budgets.

Many people have never seriously considered the difference between their needs and wants. Eating out several times a week means they will have a serious food bill. Leasing a car without reading the fine print may lead to significant penalties when the car is returned. Being unable to say no to their children may add to the family's financial burdens.

Listen to how people describe their lives. They use terms such as *house poor, car poor, possession poor,* and *cash poor.* God may not want the faithful to be rich, as some unscrupulous or theologically misdirected pastors claim, but God certainly doesn't want the faithful, through financial mismanagement, to be poor either. A pastor who doesn't talk about financial issues risks leaving the congregation uninformed of a biblical perspective and missing an important opportunity to reflect on their lives.

There are a number of financial courses offered by organizations that have a Christian perspective. When such courses are taught in the local church, people gain valuable skills that can lead to greater happiness, fewer family conflicts, and an increased ability to be generous. Such courses can also be a great way to utilize the skills and experience that church members possess. When the pastor is willing to speak about these same topics and teach a few basic financial disciplines such as goal setting, planning, saving, simple living, and generosity, a great partnership is formed.

The outcomes can be life-changing. Debt is reduced. Savings are increased. Manageable budgets are followed month after month. Over time, the benefits of living within financial boundaries become apparent. People learn to enjoy being generous and having enough money to accomplish their personal goals. Through this process, they will come to see their church more as a financial resource and less as a financial drain.

A DISCIPLESHIP ISSUE

It may seem counterintuitive, but here is what pastors and church leaders need to keep in mind: *When you talk about money you are doing people a favor. You are doing them a great service.*

It's important to remember these words, because the Reluctance is telling you to mind your own business, that money is off limits and everyone will leave your church if you preach financial management—or if, heaven forbid, you call people to sacrificial giving for the kingdom to God. Never mind the fact that Jesus talked more about money than any other topic; the Reluctance is telling you to put it off or ignore it completely. When the Reluctance delivers that message, acknowledge that it may come from many sources but it is not from the Holy Spirit.

This is a discipleship issue. If you want to help people grow in their love of Christ, if you want them to go deeper in their discipleship, if you want them to love God with their heart, soul, mind, and strength, you must talk about how they manage money. In fact, their relationship with money, wealth, and possessions will go a long way toward determining whether they relate to God or honor an idol.

Every day, people make financial decisions. The coffee they choose in the morning can be a thirty-cent homemade cup or a four-dollar designer brew at the local coffeehouse. Believe it or not, that is a discipleship decision. After all, that same person may be trying to find money in their budget to pay the rent or support the important work of the church. After that first decision about coffee, the rest of the day and week they will be in grocery stores, department stores, and restaurants; they will be considering requests of their children; they might possibly be purchasing items as expensive as a car or a home improvement. If you can help them view each decision as a reflection of their faith and love of God, they may begin to see their lives through a new lens.

Reading those words, are you suddenly feeling the Reluctance? Does such close attention to money seem too invasive or all-consuming? It shouldn't, because that's the nature of following Jesus. When Christ becomes our Lord, we give him say and sway over a multitude of decisions we make every day, and many of those decisions have price tags attached. If people learn to be thoughtful about money, then over time they may begin to practice the presence of Christ and seek the wisdom of the Holy Spirit in a host of decisions, financial and otherwise.

THE RELUCTANCE IS MESSING WITH YOU

Let me repeat: *This is a discipleship issue*. To avoid it is simply irresponsible.

When I was ordained, a bishop made me promise that I would "comfort the afflicted and afflict the comfortable." I find that when pastors afflict the comfortable, their greatest fear is the affliction they personally feel in the process. The Reluctance knows this. It knows that the easiest way to keep a pastor from talking about money is to remind them how awkward it feels.

Most pastors, by training and inclination, are people of peace. We want to resolve conflict, not create it. Typically, the prophetic part of the job is a skill we have to learn, not something that comes naturally. With a few exceptions—clergy who enjoy being prophetic about almost every possible issue—most of us don't like people to be frustrated with the message we share. And make no mistake, if you are honest about the relationship people have with money, wealth, and possessions, some of them will feel troubled and frustrated. They will probably tell you so at the back door of the sanctuary or in an e-mail after Sunday lunch is cleaned up. Some may even leave your congregation.

I'm reminded of advice offered by former pastor and author John Maxwell in a seminar I attended years ago: *You choose who you lose*. Who would you rather lose—the members who are stingy with God and don't want to reorient their financial world, or the people who tithe but need some degree of encouragement and end up leaving because you never risked providing it from the pulpit?

When people are economically able to contribute but don't give much money to the church, often they struggle with their discipleship in other areas as well. They will use a scarcity lens if they are on the church finance committee, assuming that everyone gives as little as they do. They will have low creativity in problem solving. They will have limited vision if they are in church leadership. Often these people are generous in just one area: complaints. They complain about the church, the pastor, and their fellow members. They are the first to tell the pastor that any new ministry is a bad idea, because they realize that if the church undertakes some major new effort, they will eventually be called upon to sacrifice. Sacrifice is what they are trying to avoid. So don't be surprised if they say that preaching or teaching about money is not appropriate at church.

REINFORCE THE GENEROUS

There is one group you will not lose when you speak about money in your church: the people who are generous. These people will line up to thank you for your sermon. They will never tire of the topic. They will congratulate you for having the courage to talk about it. They will thank you for your encouragement of their lifestyle. Then they will be more generous with your church, because they understand that it shares a value that is essential to the Christian life. Generosity is the brand they enjoy the most.

It's what they were looking for when they took their membership vows. Hearing a pastor's sermon or a church member's testimony on the topic is music to their ears.

Keep in mind, though, that the Reluctance whispers to them as well. No matter what their income level, generous people have so many other options. They could take a cruise, give more support to their kids, finally buy their dream car, have a larger nest egg, buy another home, or eat out more frequently. When they fill out their taxes, they look at how much money they gave away that year and ask, Was it worth it? What a difference it makes to have some word of encouragement from the church that their generosity not only honors God but that, for Christians, their giving pattern should be the norm. The Christians not following the norm are the less generous members, who contribute less than 2 percent of their income to any charitable organization, including their church. Pastors, through their silence on this topic, encourage those who are not generous and ignore those who quietly and thoughtfully honor God daily in decision after decision related to money.

Laity who serve as church leaders need to repent of their complicity in this silence. Many pastors receive both indirect signals and well-defined communication from key leaders that money is off limits. Again, these signals will usually come from church leaders who themselves are not generous and do not want to be made uncomfortable. In the generous church, leaders encourage their pastors to talk about money, because they understand that everyone in the church lives in a culture that constantly tells them to spend money and to buy newer and better. They know that people need to hear a biblical view on money that promotes an alternative and countercultural lifestyle. They also know that the pastor's willingness to talk about generosity has a direct impact on the amount of money the church will receive annually.

In the generous church, leaders know that the congregation, like any family, must talk about the hard parts of life in order to bloom and grow.

BAD NEWS, GOOD NEWS

When Christians have an extreme admiration, love, or reverence for something other than God, we call it idolatry. If we're serious about discussing money and possessions, we must name the idols people honor. Many people who are not generous simply love their idols more than they love the practice of Christian discipleship. We can easily see why. It's hard to beat the immediate gratification of owning the latest device, outfit, culinary experience, new home, second home, or third home, or of seeing our children smile when we tell them, yes, you can have that. It seems extreme even to call this idolatry, but in fact that's what it is.

Of course, some people are suffering real financial hardship because of medical bills, accidents, or unexpected job loss. Some live in poverty because they lack access to education or job training. But for most church members, when they say that they can't give money to the church—much less do something as significant as tithe—they are testifying to American idolatry. They have laid their money on the altar of materialism.

The problem usually isn't lack of money; most people in US churches are not economically poor. The problem is that they are not economically aligned to be generous. Other parts of their lives have higher priority. The interesting thing is that these priorities can actually be measured, because giving time or money is quantifiable. We can look at our spending record or calendar

40

and figure out exactly what proportion we're using to serve God. Pastors must call their congregations to do this calculation, so church members will understand, in real numbers, how faith is present or absent in their daily lives.

Idolatry and lack of generosity among some members is the bad news. But there is also good news: Many of our financial decisions honor God. People are giving food, housing, medical care, education, enrichment, transportation, communication, and a host of other good things. Pastors are wise to honor and congratulate their members for such diligence and faithfulness.

Giving is an essential part of Christian discipleship. Most of our workday is spent providing for our family members, and it's easy to overlook others who need our support. This is why sermons on vocation and financial stewardship are important. The key is to help people, as Christian disciples, to set and maintain a balance between supporting themselves and helping others.

FULFILL YOUR PASTORAL ROLE

Though pastors may hesitate to talk about money and spending, our culture does not. Make no mistake about it: every day, your church members are bombarded with marketing on their computers, TVs, radios, roadways, storefronts, newspapers, and everywhere else. Clever, well-paid advertising consultants will place ads. These professionals take their role seriously. They want us to buy things. Lots of things. New things. They don't really care if those things help us. Their goal is to increase their clients' volume of sales and profit. They don't apologize for their message. They don't worry about whether people will be offended. They don't suffer from the Reluctance. They get up every day and design the clearest, smartest, most memorable marketing campaigns possible.

The role of the church is to offer people a new way of life in Jesus Christ that will bring them hope and joy. There is no part of life that Jesus cannot save. If Jesus is to heal us from the impact of sin and show us the good life of righteousness, no part of life can be placed beyond the bounds of his Lordship. As pastors, we must provide biblically and theologically faithful sermons so that, as Paul wrote in his letter to Timothy, "they may take hold of the life that really is life" (1 Timothy 6:19b NRSV).

If we believe this is true, then we must have more passion and clarity in our messages than advertisers have in theirs. Pastors have the opportunity to offer people a better way of life that is free of debt, buyer's remorse, and squandered wealth. Through simple sermons, you may give people the encouragement they need to become generous and participate in ministry and mission. One day, when these people look back over the long arc of their life and take stock of what it all meant, such generosity will be among their most meaningful memories.

3
PLAN IT

When the plate is passed at church, people put money in for a lot of reasons. Some feel it is their duty. They understand that everything costs money and they should bear a portion of that cost through their donations. Others calculate the benefit the church currently provides to them and to members of their family, and they assign a dollar value to it. There are people who like giving and are rather indiscriminate about where they give. They might give an extra dollar for the animal shelter when buying dog food at the pet store, then give another couple of dollars to the food bank when they check out at the grocery store. They stop at lemonade stands and tell the kids to keep the change. The offering plate is just another opportunity to make another small contribution. Then there are people who are serious about their giving. They plan the percentage of their income they will give away annually and then consider what portion of that amount will go to their church. When they hear about the good work the church is doing and the lives that are blessed, they consider that good work to be their return on investment.

Though the motivations and methods of giving vary with church members, there is one thing that unites them. People give generously to churches that are generous. This is important to remember, because in churches the focus is often on holding resources rather than releasing them. This is not to say that churches are cheap but that financial prudence often moves people to avoid spending rather than decide how to allocate scarce resources. Every time the church finance committee or board meets, Reluctance pulls up a chair at the table and says, "We can't afford it," or "It will cost too much." When someone suggests encouraging the congregation in its stewardship, Reluctance warns, "You'll just offend people." Sometimes Reluctance has a whole soliloquy about what kind of church this isn't. The speech begins predictably, "We aren't a _____ church." You can fill in the blank with all sorts of words: big, rich, active, well-resourced, white-collar, young, middle-aged, or old. The message is the same: *hold tight to the money.*

GENEROSITY DOES NOT HAPPEN BY ACCIDENT

If you want to be a generous church, you have to be strategic in your generosity. Strategy enables everyone in the church to participate in the process. Plans must be considered, prayers offered, conversations shared, God's vision pursued, and decisions made about what the church can do well. This brings us back to the question of brand. What is your church about? What are you known for or want to be known for in the years ahead?

Leaders at Floris United Methodist Church, the congregation I have served for the past nineteen years, have found that two- to three-year strategic planning is effective in identifying who we uniquely want to bless at the present time. Like all churches, we have certain ministries that are ongoing and have been offered consistently over our history of 120+ years. We hold worship services, teach children the Bible and Christian beliefs, offer small groups for adults, and provide help to people in need—a list of ministries similar to many churches. In addition to our ongoing ministries, though, we periodically identify ministries to start or improve at that particular time in the life of our church, and that's where strategic planning comes in.

Let me share some of the benefits of strategic planning and how it relates to generosity.

1. A strategic plan gives people in the church the chance to talk about what is going well and what is going poorly, rather than communicating their feelings through the giving or withholding of money.
2. The plan helps people create a ministry they will support. When you open a conversation and give people a chance to share their input, they are far more likely to offer financial support for the work being discussed.
3. People like knowing the goals. Lovett Weems, who leads the Lewis Leadership Center at Wesley Theological Seminary, says that the two most important words to remember in the church are *so that*. When you tell people

what you plan to do and the reason that you plan to do it, they are far more motivated to generously offer their time, talent, and money. For example, a pastor might say, "Our church is going to assist and mentor a woman with two children who has been in a homeless shelter so that she can successfully enter transitional housing and eventually afford to rent her own apartment." Knowing the goals will create excitement in the congregation.

4. A plan can be communicated consistently over time. In many congregations, after a few months the members don't remember what the church is doing or why. If you have a strategic plan with three or four goals, you can update people on how the plan is going until it is accomplished. This allows you to show people the impact their resources are having in the church and community, and it gives them new opportunities to turn the plan into a reality.

5. A strategic plan not only tells donors what the church hopes to accomplish; it names the resources that will be required from the beginning. When people vote on the plan, they are making an initial commitment to their church, knowing that they will need to be a part of the necessary provision. This enables them to prioritize their time, talent, and money relative to the other nonprofits asking for their help.

One of the best parts of creating a strategic plan is the volume of ideas that will surface as you search for the limited number you can actually pursue. If the planning process includes multiple meetings and feedback from focus groups where ideas are shared, people will come to realize that not every idea is equally worth pursuing. This is helpful to church members who have strong opinions about their ideas. By hearing the feedback of others and realizing that many ideas did not make the final plan, people are often more willing to support the objectives that were finally included.

Strategic planning also allows church members to have hard conversations and say things that otherwise they may only have told their friends in the parking lot. For example, most churches spend about 50 percent of their funds on salary and related benefits for staff, and yet often there is no evaluation of staff members' performance or the fairness of their wages. If a staff member is seen to be ineffective, people will typically be upset about the cost of their salary to the congregation; likewise, if a staff member adds great value, people may be concerned that they are not properly compensated. People want to share these concerns and understand how churches make decisions about them. A conversation about strategic planning is typically not the forum for this conversation, but often it serves as a triage site, where the concerned member or donor can be shown where to take their questions for proper follow up.

Do Good Well

A plan is truly strategic only if it enables the church to do good well. Many churches do things that make their members feel good. Taking a food basket to a low-income family at Thanksgiving is an act of kindness that brings satisfaction to those who participate, but it does little to change the economics of the recipient. When churches consider objectives that are truly strategic, they think through issues carefully. They study the problems they want to solve. Relationships are built with experts in the field or organizations that deal with similar issues. Partnerships are forged with organizations that demonstrate expertise and competence. Plans can then be crafted that don't just do good, but do good well. Doing good well is all about the church orienting itself to fruitfulness in ministry.

I learned the phrase "do good well" from David McAllister-Wilson, president of Wesley Theological Seminary, who writes,

> The fruitfulness of our endeavors must be as important to us as the good feeling they engender in us. Fruitfulness is a key requirement of God found throughout scriptures. Time and again, God does not give points for trying or for good intentions. The barren tree is cursed and the grapevine is pruned to produce fruit. This means we must establish metrics that matter and evaluate our work.[6]

Have you ever noticed that many church buildings have a funny smell? I've found that smell to be similar even when the church size or location varies. The word I would use to describe it is *stale*. And sometimes the building is not the only thing that's stale. Take church ministries, for example. When churches do good well, it opens a window and lets in a fresh wind of the Spirit. It's amazing how invigorating people find the experience. Why should this be so? Because doing good well communicates that the church is acting in ways that are smart. People like smart. Actually, people love smart. They want to be members of smart organizations and work for smart companies. I like being around smart people, because then I feel smart by association. Even if I'm feeling a bit dull that day, I can say, *I'm with these people and they sure are smart!*

People get excited when their church shows that it's smart. When a deeply held faith in Christ comes alongside a smart way of doing ministry, it's a powerful combination. Nothing makes generosity more likely than having people believe that if money or time is given, it will be used for a good purpose and in a worthy manner. Sadly, many people do not expect the church to think strategically or do good well. Church leaders often ask donors to give resources without showing the fruit that will be produced. Whether we are educating children in the faith so they will grow up as disciples of Jesus Christ or starting a job-training class so people can find employment with benefits, the church must make a case for why its ministries are worthy of support.

Think about your church right now. What strategic goal could positively impact your ministry? What steps must you take to reach that goal? I visited a small-membership church in a rural area whose goal was to reach children in their community. One part of their plan was to renovate and update all the rooms in their building related to children's ministry. They were also going to participate in teacher training, find a new curriculum for Sunday school, and hold monthly events for children. Their plans involved much of the congregation, who got busy refinishing furniture, installing audiovisual equipment, and painting rooms. Some church members examined curriculum and developed volunteer training. Others improved child-safety policies and procedures. Step by step, the congregation was on a journey together to reach children and teach them about Christ. As a result, morale improved and generosity followed. Giving did not skyrocket, but with each new piece of the plan, donors stepped forward.

Think how valuable it would be to have a plan that the majority of your church helps to develop, knows to be strategic, and provides testimonies of transformation over time. This is the type of ministry that people will support, because they understand its importance and are involved in its planning and implementation.

TELL THEM WHAT YOU NEED

One of the most important questions that strategic plans require us to answer is what resources will be needed to reach the goals and how the church will provide them. The primary way a local church communicates these needs is through the annual budget, which will include salaries and related benefits, facility upkeep, and ministry supplies. Through the annual budget, churches identify and plan the necessary resources. This is one reason why it is so important for churches to have some sort of stewardship emphasis each year.

Most of the annual stewardship emphasis should focus on our need to give as those who follow Christ. The goal is not to raise a budget but to form Christian stewards. At the same time, the ministry budget is a useful tool to communicate the journey the congregation is taking and the exciting things it is doing in the world. If there are no exciting things to communicate, it is almost always due to a woeful lack of generosity in the congregation's life.

I don't mean a lack of generosity by the donors; I mean a lack of generosity in the life of the church that is not blessing people with its ministry. If a church is not welcoming, there is little to discuss related to hospitality. If worship services are not opportunities to invite friends and neighbors to share faith, it's no wonder there are no professions of faith. If the poor are not being lifted up, there are no such expenses to report. If a pastor is the only person visiting the sick, then the only related budget item is the pastor's salary.

On the other hand, if the church is attempting to meet people in the community, the budget will show expenses for a booth at the county fair or a face-painting session in the neighborhood. If the church is undertaking a partnership to support the local food bank, related expenses will appear as a budget line item. People understand that the ministry of the church takes resources. The question is whether those resources will be properly utilized to make a difference in the world. It should all be reflected in the annual budget.

To be effective, the annual budget for ministry should not just list expenses. It should tell the story of what the church is trying to accomplish and what strategies it is employing. In a larger church this might be a printed and electronic document. In a smaller church it could be an oral presentation on a Sunday morning. The important thing is for church members to see that planning has taken place and to understand what resources are necessary.

There is no magic in a budget or its narrative. Just because you produce the document does not mean you have raised the funds or reached the number of volunteer hours needed to implement its goals. Pastors who don't take part in raising funds or developing stewards often face disappointment that God-inspired plans are not fulfilled. Fruitful pastors and church leaders take on this challenge and work at it all through the year.

Years ago, when I was a new pastor, I heard a friend talk about a bus donated by a church member so students could be taken to retreats and activities. When I bemoaned the fact that no one ever gave me a bus, my friend stopped and said, "Did you ask anyone for a bus?" I said no, and he replied, "Well, there's your problem." I told the donor about our goal to attract middle school and high school students. I shared our plans and the goals of our retreats and activities. I showed him how important the bus would be to meet our goals. Then I asked him for the bus. Tom, your problem is that 'you don't have because you don't ask'" (James 4:2c).

In truth, my problem was far deeper than the verse he was quoting. I wouldn't have known what to do with a bus if it had dropped onto the church lawn with a full tank of gas. I didn't need a bus; I needed a vision and a ministry plan. My friend, by contrast, helped the congregation decide who they were going to reach at that particular time. He made it known that a bus would be needed in order to reach students for Christ. Then and only then did a generous donor offer the resource he needed. Suddenly the morale of the church improved. They were ministering to teenagers. And they had a bus! The generosity of one person began to inspire other people to provide meals, snacks, and time.

That is the power of the plan.

GENEROSITY IS INSPIRATIONAL

Through the year, the role of church leaders is to share stories of generosity and stewardship. The stories will inspire church members to undertake ministries that transform the church and the community.

When someone steps forward to provide a needed resource, it's an opportunity for celebration. Five new people volunteer to undergo training and lead small groups—get the word out. Thirty church members take a weekend to refurbish a home—honor them during worship with prayer and appreciation. A recently deceased church member has provided a bequest to renovate the nursery—share the news during worship as an example of a disciple who believed new generations should know the love of Christ. The key is to realize that stewardship is something we talk about and celebrate throughout the year, not just during four weeks every fall.

A good opportunity for sharing these stories is during one of the most underutilized moments of the weekly worship service: the offertory prayer. Often this prayer is repetitious and rote. Other times it is lofty and full of complex theological language. Instead, try using it to connect the generosity of God with the offering of the people. During this prayer, the pastor might mention God's many acts of grace in the lives of the congregation, along with some recent accomplishment of the church for which people offered their resources.

In all these activities, the goal is to share connections between the ministries the church has planned and the resources that are being gathered and faithfully offered.

LIFE-CHANGING GENEROSITY

The more focused on planning your church becomes, the more likely it is that you'll develop ministries that will become a part of your congregation's identity. These centerpiece ministries will bring broad participation by the congregation.

In 2000, Floris UMC founded the Child Rescue Centre (CRC) with the United Methodist Church in Sierra Leone, Africa. The CRC was created to care for children orphaned or left without support after the civil war in Sierra Leone. Over time its mission changed to care for children who are victims of child labor and trafficking. Dozens of our members have traveled to Africa to assist in the ministry. While staff members in Sierra Leone work with the children and lead the mission of the CRC, teachers and counselors from Floris and other partner churches provide staff training, summer programs, and Bible school, and they work with the children. Our church has developed important relationships with both staff and children and have celebrated as the children go into foster care or are adopted by families in the town where the CRC is located. The children are supported educationally and are provided medical care as needed, so their adoptive families do not have to carry this burden. As a result, church members have been able to follow the children's stories on into vocational school and college. Today the CRC is receiving children whose family members died during the Ebola crisis in 2014. During that crisis our church prayed weekly for our friends in Sierra Leone and helped coordinate shipments of important supplies to medical workers there.

The Child Rescue Centre is a centerpiece ministry at Floris. Our church has gained a sense of meaning and purpose in knowing the difference that ministry has made in the lives of those children in a country plagued by war, endemic poverty, and disease. The relationships we have cultivated with our friends in Sierra Leone have transformed the ways we see our faith in Christ. Over the years, hundreds of people have generously given their time, abilities, and money to support this ministry. We celebrate their generosity, but at the same time, leaders in our church know that this ministry and a few others like it in our congregation represent a large unfunded liability to our church. To sustain this ministry for the next ten years will take a great deal of money and further effort on the part of our members. For this reason, we have had to be very strategic in considering requests to expand this ministry. It is not hard to start a significant ministry; it is difficult to sustain one for over ten years. This is another reason that strategic plans are needed.

Some of your ministry may be funded beyond the church budget through the use of significant fund-raisers, enabling people in the community to participate in the good you are doing in the world. Each year, we hold a golf tournament for the Child Rescue Centre through our nonprofit organization, Helping Children Worldwide. By running the event through the nonprofit, corporations can sponsor the tournament and make larger donations. Our church members seek corporate and business donations from their friends in the community who may not even go to church. At the dinner following the tournament we give out awards, thank everyone profusely, and share pictures and stories of the work of the CRC. Some years we have had former residents of the CRC tell our donors how their contributions changed their lives through education, medical care, and the provision of a home.

The benefits of a centerpiece ministry are numerous. Some of the golfers and donors become interested in our congregation, because nothing interests people in a church more than stories of lives changed through generosity. People who came just to play golf sometimes express a desire to give other gifts, such as their time or expertise. Others are willing to give financial contributions beyond the golf tournament. Though many simply play golf, enjoy the meal, and go home, some become future partners in the ministry. Remember that most people in your community do not give more than 1 or 2 percent of their income to any charitable cause. This means that if you are doing something that interests them, they may have the capacity to assist you. That connection may be an entry point into an important conversation about the faith in Christ that motivates your good work. Generosity is an effective tool in evangelism, because it speaks to the sincerity and sacrifice inherent in the Christian faith. People are looking for sincere forms of faith in the world.

I am not suggesting that the church should hold fund-raiser after fund-raiser to support its ministry. Some churches spend so much time on flea markets, Brunswick stew sales, and church suppers that they have no energy or time left for ministry. However, if there is an important ministry that you need to sustain, and if the fund-raising activity itself will create a positive word in your community about your church, it may be a worthwhile activity. Of course, this is only true if the event, like our golf tournament, can raise enough money to make a significant contribution to the ministry it seeks to sustain. The focus of the fund-raising cannot be the survival of the congregation; it must be an opportunity for the community to join the church in blessing the world. This is an important calculation, because small fund-raisers done frequently are like a dog chasing its tail: There's a lot of activity, but before long you start to wonder, What's the point?

THROUGHOUT THE YEAR

Certain seasons are strategic in the stewardship ministry of the church. The most obvious are Advent and Christmas. I learned about changing the focus of Advent and Christmas from Mike Slaughter of Ginghamsburg Church, whose powerful ministry helped lead our church members to reconsider the meaning of Christmas. A full treatment of this subject can be found in Mike's book, *Christmas Is Not Your Birthday* (Abingdon Press, 2011).

Here I want to say that to show you are a generous church, the most important thing you can do each year is give away your entire Christmas Eve offering to a worthy cause as part of your strategic plan. You can fund an entire ministry from that one offering by surprising people who attend church only on the high holy days of Christmas and Easter, along with those who never attend church but are visiting their relatives at the holiday. When these visitors hear that the church is not keeping a dollar of the special offering, but rather is honoring the birth of Christ by caring for the poor and vulnerable, they see the church as an organization with integrity and credibility, and they often give accordingly.

Giving away the Christmas Eve offering has another benefit. It allows the pastor to speak to the congregation during a time when people are making final year-end contribution decisions before the December 31 tax deadline. The pastor and lay leadership can communicate that the special offering can only be given away if church members complete their normal support of the budget. Donations must be completed to the budget and not redirected on Christmas Eve.

If the Christmas Eve offering is handled in this way, it becomes a sacrificial gift to honor and celebrate the birth of the Savior. It is an appropriate response to the generosity of God in Jesus' birth. For people who are tired of all the Christmas hype being pushed by the American marketing machine, the offering can transform the celebration of Christmas. Every year, our leaders are thanked by visitors and church members alike, who say that the Christmas Eve offering is one of the most special moments of their annual celebration.

Likewise, the Advent season becomes a time when we help people find ways to bless others in the community. We reach out to our community partners and make it easy for our members to buy gifts for children, supplies for local shelters, and books for the local elementary school. As a result, members find the season more meaningful, they learn about needs in the community, they help bless the vulnerable, and they practice generosity. Advent giving brings light and joy to a month that is often portrayed as overwhelming in activity and shrouded in consumerism.

Some readers may hear Reluctance saying that these ideas will never work in their church. Giving away a year-end offering will mean a budget deficit. Encouraging small acts of generosity will hurt the church budget. On and on, Reluctance builds its case for closing our fists, while Christ calls us to open our arms and give generously.

Here is the truth: Whatever the time of year, people will give sacrificially to generous churches. Tell that to congregational leaders who guard the treasury like Ebenezer Scrooge in his counting house before the ghosts showed up. Tell that, in fact, to everyone, because it turns out that communicating your strategic plan is as important as developing it in the first place. The key to overcoming Reluctance is to develop a diligent plan of communication throughout the year. That is what we will talk about next.

4

COMMUNICATE IT

Leaders of the generous church learn how to talk about money and about the need for volunteers and spiritual gifts for ministry throughout the year. The disciplined stewardship that leads to generosity from church members must be communicated every month for twelve months, not just endured for a couple of weeks in October or November.

RELUCTANCE GIVES TERRIBLE ADVICE

For pastors, preaching and talking about money, possessions, and wealth should be the rule, not the exception. Sadly, many pastors talk about money only when it is absolutely necessary.

Reluctance wants us to treat discussions of money in the church like lifeboats on a cruise ship: pull them out only when the ship is going down. To do otherwise will disturb the passengers and create anxiety. In this view, sermons on generosity are perceived as negative, only to be used when panic sets in. They are like warning messages to abandon ship.

This approach works against vital ministry, which requires both time and money. Churches whose finances are always tight find themselves in a downward spiral of scarcity. It becomes increasingly difficult to pay the pastor's salary, keep up the building, and pay the utilities. The less the church does, the less generous it appears, and the less the people feel motivated to give. No one wants to support what is perceived to be a sinking organization. That's why pastors and church leaders must share good news on an ongoing basis, in order to enliven the congregation. The best way to do this is to tell the story of the congregation's generosity.

Reluctance has odd theories about discussing generosity and finances in the church. First it will tell you to do nothing. Be silent about all things financial. Then, when giving is down and the budget is tight, it will tell you to send out an urgent SOS to everyone. This often takes the form of one gloomy report after another saying how far behind the church is financially. Or it might show up as painful weekly announcements in the bulletin reporting how much money the church needs and how much it received last week, along with negative totals from January to October. Never mind that year after year in healthy congregations, the finances magically break even around November and December, when people do their year-end giving. Reluctance tells you that there is no better way to inspire sacrificial giving than by repeating bad news.

Tell Reluctance that it is wrong. What people want is a real picture of what is needed and the good news of what is happening in their church. And every church has some good news.

There are many ways to communicate that good news so people will feel excited about their church. Used consistently, these communications portray generosity and encourage generosity. Pastors who focus on these areas will soon find that Reluctance cannot build a worthy case for silence and inaction. By communicating well, pastors will enjoy building up their congregations and sharing appreciation for people whose discipleship is evidenced in their daily lives. Good news is contagious, and people like to share it with others.

SHARE GOOD NEWS

1. Stories

Last summer a woman in our church sent me an e-mail thanking the church for holding Vacation Bible School. Her son learned about God's power during VBS. He heard songs on that theme by listening to a CD that each child took home. His mom said that previously her son had not connected well with God and faith. She reported,

> But this week at VBS something clicked for him! He has been talking about God and all the powers God has. He has been making books about God with Bible verses from [his week at VBS]. He has been requesting the "God songs" in the car. He even conquered a fear of jumping off the diving board and later told me he was able to do it by trusting in God. Makes my heart so happy. So thank you!

61

That is a story that needs to be told. Everything that happened in VBS took financial resources, from the building to the curriculum. People gave their time and talent to the effort. Sharing a story like this one—whether in a sermon or an e-mailed newsletter to thank VBS volunteers—enables people to see the value of the church's ministry and the reasons they are wise to invest in it. There are plenty of stories like this around your church.

One key to sharing a story such as this one is to be particular and specific. Imagine that a pastor says in her sermon, "This week our children learned about God's power. That lesson will enable them to face their fears in life." Put in this way, the point will roll right over the congregation on its way out the front door. Now imagine the pastor saying, "I want to tell you about a young man in our congregation who faced his fears because of what you did to support our Vacation Bible School." She reads the e-mail from the child's mother, then asks those who assisted in VBS to stand up and be thanked by the congregation. The pastor goes on to share her appreciation for the financial support and prayers offered by others who were not able to volunteer. Soon everyone in the worship service feels connected to the success of that child. Now a case has been made that the church is having an impact. If this year's VBS touched one child this way, how might it have affected others who attended?

Besides being specific, be sure to show variety, sharing stories about many different ministry areas. Different church members will be excited about different areas of the life of the church. Has someone recently been baptized? Those who want to see the church make disciples will be pleased to hear it. Did a mission team just return from rebuilding homes after a hurricane? Share stories about who they met and what they did. Are you holding the first confirmation class offered in several years? Whether it has three participants or thirty, people will be glad to hear about it. Have the children learned a new Bible story? Invite them to share a presentation with the congregation. Has a group taken a prayer blanket to the hospital for a sick church member? Talk about what it meant to both the patient and the group. Hearing about every aspect of the church's ministry will encourage your members to invest in the church.

2. Numbers

Numbers have a bad reputation. When asked to report numbers, church leaders sometimes downplay it as just a "numbers game." But numbers represent lives touched and situations changed. They help people understand what is going well and to what extent the church is accomplishing its mission. Just as personal accounts tell the story of the one person, numbers tell the story of the many.

The first churches I served were small. One had about thirty-five people in attendance. After a year, there were thirty-nine people, an addition of four. I told people how excited I was that worship attendance had grown by 10 percent that year. I did some research and found that a 10-percent growth rate was higher than any of the large churches in our area. That made us one of the fastest-growing churches by percentage in our region. People were excited by that news, even though they understood that it was only four people. They also understood that for many years that church had had no growth at all. So a 10 percent increase was good news, and good news is exciting. Once they knew the numbers, people began to feel like part of a more vital congregation. When the church is seen as alive and growing, people are far more likely to invite their friends to attend worship services or other events.

The numbers don't have to be big, just relevant. Imagine the information below shared during a sermon, before the offering, or in the announcements:

- We have three new babies in the nursery and had to buy two cribs to accommodate them.
- Last year we had eighteen students at the opening event for our high school ministry. This fall we had twenty-five, and we have challenged them to bring a friend next week.
- Ten of our members invited a friend to church in December. I'm so grateful to be part of a church that wants others to know the love of Christ.

Numbers help show that the Holy Spirit is at work among us. In your church, there are some people who are motivated by numbers more than stories. These members want to know that their money has been invested well and is making an impact. For them, numbers are welcomed as a form of testimony.

3. Outcomes

Let people know how things turned out. The church I serve, along with other congregations, raised funds to provide an ambulance for Ebola patients in Sierra Leone. People heard about the need and gave to it. They were excited to realize that when the ambulance arrived, it doubled the number of Ebola ambulances in the district where it served. They were pleased when they saw pictures of the new ambulance in use by medical personnel at a church hospital. They were even more excited when they heard a story of individuals who made it to the treatment center because the ambulance was available. At different points during the Ebola crisis, we announced how the ambulance was used and how many people had been transported because of it.

After the crisis abated in Sierra Leone, we made sure to talk about how the ambulance was cleaned and refurbished for other uses, such as transporting pregnant women from their villages to the hospital in emergencies. None of these updates took very long to share. Sometimes we had a slide to show people. Other times it was a quick note in the weekly electronic newsletter or before the offering in worship. When you share outcomes, you honor people who donate time, effort, and money to a good cause and let them know that their investment had a significant return.

Sharing outcomes is especially important when you are working on a strategic plan. People need to be reminded repeatedly what the church is trying to accomplish and what progress has been made. Updates allow you to do this in a positive way. Rather than saying, "Let me go over this again," you might say, "I want to give you a quick update on where we are in our strategic plan. You'll recall we had four objectives. Here is our progress to date."

A quick report such as this one brings everyone up to speed and gently reminds them how much the church needs their time and talent. This is in contrast to other nonprofits that seek donations but are too large to connect a specific donation to a specific need or individual whom it served.

Every donor wants a George Bailey moment. Do you remember the movie *It's a Wonderful Life*? When Clarence the angel took George Bailey around Bedford Falls to see what the town would have been like if George had not been born, Clarence gave him a great gift. Scene by scene, person by person, George could see what his contributions of time, talent, and money had done for the town and the people in it.

When you share outcomes of people's work and donations, you become Clarence the angel. If someone's life has been blessed, let people know. If your church partners with an organization doing good work, show your members. Don't assume they are making all the connections on their own. Sharing outcomes enables you to connect the dots between the donor and the result.

4. Testimonies

When people share what Christ is doing in their lives or how being part of the church has enabled them to grow in their faith, their testimonies are powerful.

Testimonies come in many forms. They can be delivered orally during worship, in which case you should give people a time limit and ask them to write out their comments. Help them understand their topic and how they can best convey their message. Explain how their remarks fit into the other elements of worship.

Testimonies can also be prerecorded on video, sometimes using a camera as simple as the one on your phone. With some basic editing techniques, the video can be tailored to the desired length. But be careful when you do this. The rule of thumb is that people will forgive bad images but need good audio or subtitles so they can understand what is being said. If people don't feel comfortable using video, their testimony can take the form of a written note in the church bulletin, newsletter, or social media.

Whatever form the testimony takes, the goal is to show people that their church ministry is important in the community and represents a worthy investment of their time and money. Sometimes the testimony is not about ministry but about generosity as an act of discipleship. When you find people being generous, celebrate it so others will be motivated and inspired.

While writing this chapter I received an e-mail from a church member about Jack, a boy in our congregation who was about to turn nine years old. Jack asked his friends not to bring gifts to his birthday party but to bring donations for the Floris Guest House, a program at our church for persons who are homeless. Here is a portion of the birthday invitation:

> Jack would like to use his birthday as an opportunity to support a charity in our area. He is asking anyone that would have brought him a gift to consider instead supporting the Floris Guest House. The Floris Guest House is a program in conjunction with FACETS (Fairfax Area Christian Emergency Transitional Services) where Floris United Methodist Church will house a hypothermia shelter this January. To support this effort, Floris is requesting gift card donations for any local gas stations, fast food restaurants as well as general retail cards in order to supply the residents with any needed shoes & clothing. If you would be willing to support this effort, Jack would be very grateful. Thank you!

With the permission of Jack and his parents, I will share this note with the congregation. I don't even have to use his name. Just knowing that a child in our church is this generous will motivate others to generosity. And consider what Jack is doing for his church. Not only will his request bring gifts for people in need; the families of his friends will identify our church with a generous life. Jack's testimony is both a generous gift and an opportunity for evangelism.

Don't limit testimonies to special occasions. Seek out volunteers who have served over a long period of time and show appreciation to them. This will represent a testimony of their commitment to Christ. Notice acts of kindness and, with permission, share them with the church. Make sure to tell stories about generosity of any size. Some churches only recognize generosity when they are sharing the good news of a major gift or naming the new wing of a building. These big donations are important, but the church must be careful not to focus on the size of the gift. Generosity is not about financial ability or even age. It is a virtue shared by all sorts of people in all kinds of economic conditions. Generous people enjoy hearing stories of others giving in a variety of ways.

Where can your church do a better job of communicating generosity? How can you enable your members tell their stories so others will be excited about the church's ministry? Nothing is more credible than the firsthand testimony of people in your church.

5. Financial Updates

As you hold finance committee and church board meetings through the year, give your congregation feedback about how the church is doing financially by writing a paragraph in the church newsletter or by enclosing such information in quarterly statements. Don't just give the numbers; interpret them so people will understand the importance of their donations to the church's ministry.

Try to avoid those fervent pleas for money that sound as though the ship is sinking. Such pleas only motivate in the short term and quickly create donor fatigue. What people want to know is how money is being managed, how lives are being impacted, and what leaders are doing. They want to make sure the church is accomplishing a vital ministry while attending to good financial practices. Pay attention to the tone of your writing. "I want you to know where we are financially at this time" sounds so much better than "I am writing because we have a desperate need!"

When clergy and laity unite to lead the congregation in an ongoing conversation about money in their personal lives and in their life together as a church, great things begin to happen. Generosity becomes a goal connected to the mission and ministry of the church. Church members align their finances with that goal and make generosity a personal value that is lived out daily. In the process, the church community learns to surrender their lives to Christ in a way that is normative to those who followed Christ in the Bible and throughout church history.

6. Tell the Community

Community newspapers and websites are always on the hunt for good human-interest stories. If you call them and share some act of generosity in the church, they are often willing to send out a reporter or have you prepare an article for their use.

Some Christians don't like to seek out publicity, recalling that Jesus told his disciples, "Be careful that you don't practice your religion in front of people to draw their attention. If you do, you will have no reward from your Father who is in heaven" (Matthew 6:1). Keeping Jesus' words in mind, if you are doing a generous act for the sole purpose of publicity, it may be better not to call the reporter. But if your goal is to share ways your faith in Christ motivates you to bless others, it amounts to public testimony and is an effective form of evangelism. People in your community are far more likely to attend your church if they hear that it's generous, and they will not hear it unless you tell them. Sharing acts of generosity also breaks the prevailing stereotypes found in movies and TV of Christians who are hypocritical and self-serving.

A reputation for generosity will create a positive "buzz" about your church. Rev. Kirk Nave, pastor of Braddock Street United Methodist Church in Winchester, Virginia, helped me see the value of building a community reputation. Some of his students and their parents were participating in a community prayer event at their school on the National Day of Prayer. When a woman in the crowd asked them where they went to church, they said, "Braddock Street United Methodist." The woman replied, "Oh, that's the church that does so much for the community! And your youth are always doing some kind of mission project. Your church sounds like an awesome group of people!"

I'll bet that if the woman had a friend looking for a congregation to visit and lived near the church, she might refer them to Braddock Street, even though she isn't a member there. Kirk tells me that he hears those comments repeated fairly often in different ways around their town. Obviously they are doing a great of job building a reputation for generosity. It's a key reason the church is vital and attracting new members.

7. Say Thanks

Another powerful way to communicate generosity is simply to say thanks. We all know we should thank people, but we rarely get the chance to do so during the course of a year. Make saying thanks a part of your church identity. There are several ways to do this.

Send out quarterly statements showing how much the congregation gave. Include a note of appreciation along with a few stories of what has been accomplished recently or how the strategic plan is going. Send the statement to everyone who contributes any sum of money to your church. The church is virtually the only nonprofit that doesn't regularly thank people for their donations. This may be one reason it has lost such a significant percentage of the total dollars donated in the United States in recent years.

Make a list of one or two people you can write to and thank each week for acts of generosity involving time, talent, or money. Send these notes indiscriminately. When you see someone you want to thank, jot down their name and the reason at the time you see it. Make a point of noticing people who fix things, volunteer in the office, maintain the building, participate in meetings, or serve in the nursery. Buy some small stationary cards. You don't need to write a page of thanks. If the note is three to four sentences long, you are far more likely to write it and send it than if you're trying to fill a page. Two notes of gratitude a week is an achievable goal. Think of it—over the course of twelve months, that adds up to 104 notes of appreciation.

When you thank people in this way, you can't be accused of thanking only those who give the largest donations. The best part is that there's a direct link between the practice of gratitude and the practice of generosity. When you are generous with appreciation, you will find that people will be generous in return. They will know they are valued. They will enjoy bringing value to the congregation's ministry. And who knows? Once you start thanking people, you may have a personal revival of gratitude that will do a lot for your own personal life!

At the beginning of December, send a small thank-you gift to your top donors—perhaps the top 10 percent of them. Remember, if you follow the advice in this chapter, you will have been thanking all your donors regularly. Here I want to affirm two truths. First, every donation is important to the life of your church, no matter what its size or source. Second, there are people in your church who give larger sums of money and whose generosity is indispensable to the church budget. This is the group that you can thank in a more personal way.

If the notion of thanking people for larger financial donations is troublesome to you, take a moment and write out the names of people who give the largest amounts of time to your church. Now make a list of people who have unique talents or skills that your church could not afford if you had to pay for them. Send the top 10 percent of these generous people a small gift as well.

The gift should be private and delivered with little fanfare. Through the year I look for an affordable book that might help people grow in their life in Christ. The book is typically one that I have read and that enriched my faith. My note will tell them why I chose the book and what I hope they will get out of it. One year I was in Jerusalem and found olive wood Christmas ornaments. I bought enough to give one to each of our top donors. It was a small gift, but people appreciated the fact that I thought of them while on a trip to consider the life of Christ. Another year, I bought small bone crosses in a Sierra Leone market while on a mission trip. In each case, explaining the context of the gift made it more personal. My note always tells recipients what a difference their gifts make to the ministry of our church and clearly says thanks.

Even as I type this suggestion, I can feel Reluctance moving to block this idea. Its questions are immediate:

Q: *What will other church members think about this practice?*

A: I don't plan on telling them, and I don't think others will either. In the letter I identify recipients as a family in the top 10 percent of our contributors or someone with a unique talent. I have never had anyone walk around the church sharing that information with others. But I have had people tell me how much it meant to them that their generosity was acknowledged and appreciated.

Q: Should the pastor even know how much people give? Won't it change their relationship?

A: I once told a pastor friend that I didn't want to know how much people gave, fearing that I would favor some people. He replied, "If you found out they were once in prison, would that change how you saw them? If they said they were getting a divorce, would you judge and reject them? Why do you feel you can handle all sorts of private information but not level of giving?" I was immediately convinced and have been ever since. In fact, I've found that by sending a small token of appreciation and a note of thanks, I've opened up many pastoral conversations over the years. These conversations often have been beneficial to the church member and have helped me understand the burden of decision-making felt by many people who enjoy greater resources or who are serious about generosity.

Q: Shouldn't people just give without needing to be thanked?

A: Of course they should, and they do. But don't we all need encouragement? Jesus tells us we might one day hear the voice of our Creator say, "Well done, good and faithful servant." That sounds like something that would be pleasant to experience. Why wait for eternity when we can encourage and appreciate each other right now?

8. Listen

Everyone has reasons for giving. The reasons vary with the person or the family. People also have different reasons for donating to your church. How can you discover those reasons? By listening.

Listen first for people who enjoy giving to your church or in the community. Here again, "giving" includes time, expertise, and financial resources. When you hear people express joy in an act of generosity, ask them to tell you more.

Of course, Reluctance will whisper that giving is personal and you shouldn't ask about it. But I'll tell you a secret: truly generous people don't like to draw attention to their giving, but they really enjoy talking about the happiness it brings them. They don't have many opportunities to talk about it, so they typically are more than happy to schedule time over lunch. (Make sure you buy the meal!) Or you may just stop by their home to talk about what motivates their giving. By doing so, you will discover insights about giving that will inform your communications about this topic.

Put together two sets of questions that might help you in this conversation. The first set is about the general topic of generosity in their lives. Here are a few possibilities:

- Why do you give?
- Who taught you to be generous?
- What is the kindest way someone was generous to you?
- If you had to share one or two acts of generosity that you offered a person or an organization that brought you the most joy, what would they be?
- How do you decide where to donate your time or money?
- How long has giving been a habit in your life?
- What event led you to become a generous person?

Then, after talking about the general topic of generosity, find out why they give to your church specifically. When people donate funds to the ministry of your congregation, they are deciding not to give those dollars to many other worthy nonprofit organizations. Knowing why they give to your church instead will enable you to understand why they think it's important. The more such conversations you have, the more you will understand what people like about your church "brand" and what distinctive aspects of the church ministry you should sustain over time. This information will assist you in many ways as a leader.

Develop a second set of questions about giving to your church specifically. Here are some possibilities:

- Why do you give to our church?
- Who taught you to contribute to the church?
- When did you start supporting the church, and what led you to see that as a good idea?
- What about our church brings you the most joy?
- What about our church concerns you the most?
- If we had to scale back our ministry, what would you want to make sure we did not give up?
- In what ways do you think our church is most helpful to its members?
- What are the most effective ways we bless the community and why?

Listen carefully, and take notes if it helps you. Holding these conversations is one of the best ways to demonstrate that you don't just see the donor as an ATM for your church but as a valued ministry partner whose insights are helpful to church leaders.

During these conversations, you'll probably find that serious donors will want to know that your church employs the best practices for handling and accounting for its funds. Managing the money and the decision-making processes is especially important to people who are serious about generosity. In fact, you'll find that the more people give, the more they will want to know that the church handles their funds professionally.

5

MANAGE IT

TIME AND MONEY

The two main contributions people make to churches are time and money. Along with time, people give their spiritual gifts, education, and unique skills. But Reluctance has a way of telling church leaders that it is better to ask for a person's time than their money. It says that a request for money will be off-putting and offensive, while a request for time is simply an opportunity to help out a good cause.

One might get the idea that time is less valuable than money. Nothing could be further from the truth. Given a choice, most people would far rather donate money than time. Time is fixed: you can't make more of it or get it back. Money is variable: you can increase your income by taking a new job with a higher salary or working a second job on weekends.

However, both time and money are valuable, and most people wish they had a bit more of each. That is why generous churches think carefully about how to ask for each of them.

Let's start with six keys to recruiting and managing the time that people generously offer.

1. Create a Culture of Servanthood

The disciples may have been muddled about Jesus' message, but he was crystal clear. The Gospel of Mark recalls the moment Jesus predicted his death. Though the disciples did not understand what he was talking about and were afraid to ask for clarification, they somehow felt inspired to argue with each other about who was the greatest disciple. What a fun bunch they must have been, each making his own case for personal greatness as they made their way across the hills and valleys of Galilee. For miles they walked together, describing questions they had gotten right and good things they had done. ("And another good thing about me is my humility.")

When they got to the village of Capernaum, Jesus sat down wearily and asked, "What were you arguing about during the journey?" (Mark 9:33). It was a question that was not a question. And they all knew it. No one responded. We can imagine what happened. There was an embarrassed silence and suddenly a lot of interest in the condition of their sandals. One of the disciples cleared his throat. Someone coughed. A couple of them actually blushed. Then Mark recounts, "He sat down, called the Twelve, and said to them, 'Whoever wants to be first must be least of all and the servant of all'" (Mark 9:35).

This one sentence captures so much of what Jesus had been trying to teach his followers the entire time they were with him. They had spent hundreds of hours together, and they still did not understand the main thing.

Not much has changed. Even today Jesus is trying to help us understand the message: until we are servants, we will never find the greatness of God's kingdom. A good servant is someone who revels in the master's joy. A good servant finds satisfaction in offering their best when someone provides for their needs. A good servant looks for ways to be fully employed doing the master's work.

Pastors and church leaders in our time must understand: your church will become generous when servanthood is the norm and not the exception. When people long to serve God, the church has vitality and good things happen. When people complain about how the church isn't meeting their own needs, you can order the casket. That congregation will be dead in no time. Jesus said you have to lose your life to find it. It's that simple. People trying to keep their life by holding tightly to their time and money will end up losing a chance to experience the good that God has in store for them.

The role of the pastor and key leaders in the congregation is to make servanthood the culture of the church. The concept has to be explained, modeled, illustrated, celebrated, and called out over and over again. Unless servanthood permeates the congregation like dye on fabric, the church will never truly be generous. Make no mistake: in ways large and small, we must call people to serve.

When servanthood pervades every ministry area of the church, generosity of spirit will begin to overflow, and joy will follow. Look for moments to call people to servanthood.

2. Take Responsibility

Pastors have to take some responsibility in the process of recruiting volunteers. For ministry leaders or staff who need volunteers, imagine how helpful it is when the pastor is willing to speak about that need during announcements, pray for volunteers during worship, or preach about servanthood.

Many pastors feel that the task of recruitment is beneath the dignity of a sermon. Their job is to exegete the text and remind people of the Bible's timeless truths. But those who want to see generosity take hold understand that the entire congregation benefits if they can preach or otherwise inspire people to serve and then offer specific ways to get involved. This type of preaching and encouragement has a tangible effect on church members.

One way to get started is to look at the church calendar to see when volunteers need to be recruited. For example, the spring is often a good time to ask people to serve in the fall as teachers and small-group leaders. If you wait until the late summer or September, people may already have made other commitments. The fall may be a time to talk about servanthood, as church leaders, committee members, and team members are considered for the coming year. Every congregation has seasons and cycles that will be easily recognized by the pastor.

Ask church leaders what help they need in finding people to serve in the congregation. If Reluctance is telling you that people don't want to be bothered and so you shouldn't push too hard, remember that asking is one of the key ways you serve the church. Then do it.

3. Make It Easy

If you want people to offer their time and talents, give them a fast and easy way to sign up. Use the options that best fit your congregation. For some churches this will be sign-up sheets at the back of the sanctuary. Other churches will ask members to go to the church website, which will take their information and send reminders about their area of service. There are many other options including bulletin inserts, perforated tabs on the bulletin that can be torn off and placed in the offering plate, and display tables where ministry leaders can introduce themselves and answer questions.

Here is what does not work: a call for help with no clear way to gather information or sign up. This is especially the case for those new to the congregation. When the announcement ends in a wistful *Talk to Sandy, she's been leading this for years*, new people will have no way of knowing who Sandy is, and enthusiasm will wane. Not only will volunteers fail to sign up but people will be frustrated that they can't generously give the time they would like to offer.

4. Clarify

Treat the volunteer's time with interest and respect. Let people know how much time they're being asked to give on a weekly or monthly basis. And don't underestimate. Years ago I asked a finance committee member, Craig, to lead that team. I told him it would take just a few hours a month. After he agreed, Craig discovered it actually took several hours a week. He was incredibly generous with his time and skills when the church needed him, and over time we found others to help carry the load. But Craig still reminds me today, over a decade later, that I made the job sound like a small task rather than the substantial commitment it turned out to be.

When preparing a description of volunteer needs, talk to current volunteers to find out how much time their ministry takes. Ask them for a paragraph or two describing what they do and what gifts and abilities are necessary. Include the desired term of service. Some tasks are brief, while others require a commitment of more than a year. If you spell out the term of service, you will lessen people's fear that they will be volunteering until the end of time. You will also give them a starting point for discussion if they want to ask for a shorter term of service.

If you're clear about needs and scope of responsibility, you'll be letting prospective volunteers know you appreciate their time is limited, and you'll reinforce the impression that you are organized. People like to be part of a church that demonstrates care of the people who serve.

5. Offer Training and Support

Give some form of training, even if it is just a brief orientation to the task and its importance. Help people understand not only what they will be doing but why they are doing it. Tell them who will be enriched by their task and how it serves God's purposes.

For volunteer tasks that require more formal training, you can often arrange it in conjunction with other churches. For instance, if you don't have enough volunteers in a teaching ministry to support your own training event, contact another church and offer a workshop together. Training events provide information that volunteers need. Training also communicates that the task is important enough for the church to invest in the volunteers.

After the initial training, don't forget to provide ongoing support. This could include checking in with people to make sure they have the supplies they need and some assistance in problem solving for issues that inevitably arise. Follow-up can be done through a quarterly phone call to ask people how they are doing, find out whether they enjoy their area of service, discover how the church can assist them, and thank them for their service.

6. Say Thanks

Show your appreciation to volunteers early and often. Tell them about it when you see them at the church or in the community. Send them messages on social media. Write them notes. Recognize them in worship or at other events. Hold a year-end dinner with honors or awards: most creative teacher, most likely to make a crying baby smile, and others. The point is that showing appreciation does not have to cost money or be complicated. Just remember that for most people, time is more valuable than money, and give thanks accordingly.

When a term of service ends, sit down with the volunteer and tell them how grateful you are. Recall some ways they made a difference at the church. And make sure to ask them where God's calling is leading them next. Service not an event or season. It is a lifestyle.

INVESTOR CONFIDENCE

Just as you have to manage the investment of time, you also must carefully manage the process of financial donations. The way you manage money and the information that you share with your donors will build investor confidence. After all, people are not just giving to your church; they truly are investing in it. They want to know not just that their money is well-used but that it's well-managed until it is spent. People give more to organizations that they trust, and a good way to build trust is to follow best practices in handling and dispersing funds.

I once knew of a church that handled the offering this way: A trusted married couple in the church gathered up the offering and placed it in a cloth bag. They took the bag home with them after the church service. They sorted the cash, recorded checks, and tallied the offering while watching their favorite football team on Sunday afternoon. On Monday, the offering was delivered to the church secretary, who validated their numbers and took the money to the bank for deposit.

The church members didn't have a problem with this process, because most of the members had known the couple since they were children. Nor did anyone express concern about wrongdoing. Fortunately for the church, the couple was trustworthy. But can you imagine hearing about this process if you were a new member trying to decide whether to invest funds in the life of the church?

Just as there are keys to managing the time that people generously offer, there also are keys and good practices to follow with financial contributions.

1. Handling the Weekly Offering.

The weekly offering is best counted by teams of two or three people who are unrelated to each other and who rotate monthly. These teams sort the bills, tally the checks, and create a collections log for that week.

The weekly offering should be placed in a secure location. A small safe in a discreet location is best for this purpose, unless you can take it directly to the bank. Most churches have the treasurer count the offering a second time on Monday, so a small safe is necessary.

Set up a way that money can be noted and secured if people bring checks or cash at an odd time, such as their payment for a child's retreat or their offering when they missed a Sunday. A safe with a rolling drum on top is very useful, so the pastor, staff, or church members don't ever have to hold money.

It's also helpful if the pastor doesn't know the combination to the safe. The best policy for clergy is never physically to touch money but simply to know where people can take it for safekeeping.

2. Budgeting

When church leaders compute the budget, spend some time considering how much money will be spent and received each month. Some expenses are seasonal. These should be identified so that you are ready for them when they arrive. Have proper codes for expenses so that you can see at the end of the year exactly where all the money went.

Set up expense categories specific enough that you can understand how money is being used for your ministry and that it won't be hidden in larger categories that will create confusion. Paper for the copier, for instance, might be its own category rather than being lumped in "office supplies." That way you will notice if the copier is being used at an unexpectedly high rate or if usage is comparable to years past.

Church members with concerns about the budget will want to know that it is being monitored closely to ensure excellent stewardship. Demonstrate that you share this value by planning, executing, and reporting a midyear budget reforecast. A midyear reforecast will enable the finance committee or church council to reallocate funds within the budget, so concerned members will know that the church won't risk being in a deficit if offerings run short.

Some ministries may not need all their funds, while some may need additional funds to support a strategic goal or new opportunity that has presented itself. A midyear reforecast enables the church to have a conversation about these adjustments in a calm and productive way. Dealing with the adjustments midyear rather than at the end of the year will let the congregation know the budget is based on actual income and expenditures over the course of the year, and that the church is handling financial contributions in an open, effective, timely way.

3. Good Reporting

It's important for the church to understand and report financial contributions and when they are made. Church revenue does not come in twelve equal amounts; knowing your congregation's distinct pattern is essential if you want to forecast future revenue and lower anxiety. This information will enable your church to project its total annual income by midyear, then complete a budget reforecast that will help you arrive on budget at year end.

At our church, it's been helpful to use a three-year historical receipts model in forecasting and reporting what percentage of our budget tends to arrive in a given month. If you're not sure how to do this, use "The Congregational Giving Profile," a resource you can find at the Lewis Center at Wesley Theological Seminary (http://www.churchleadership.com/cgp). A three-year receipts model, combined with financial reports related to expenditures, will enable you to see where money is going and how fast it is being spent.

Good reporting enables you to avoid fourth-quarter surprises that turn into desperate pleas to the congregation. Having this type of information will be especially helpful when a member of your congregation expresses concern about the financial health of the church. When that happens, you'll be able to show three years' worth of financial data, along with an understanding of what income percentage historically comes in each month. Church members will be grateful for the information and reassured about the careful work of the treasurer and finance committee.

When a church demonstrates competence with financial analysis, donors will be far more likely to give with confidence.

4. Making It Easy to Give

If you want your church to become more generous, offer new ways for people to give to the church. Arrange for automatic drafts from the donor's checking account. Set up online giving for debit or credit cards through your website or through text messages from the donor's cell phone. Businesses of all sizes have been using these methods for years and have enjoyed the rewards of customers finding it easier to pay their bills in an easy and timely way. When you make giving easier for your donors, you make income more dependable for your church.

Think of how the world has changed in terms of commerce in just a few generations. Seventy years ago, when my father was a boy and went to church with his parents, they put cash in the offering plate. In fact, my grandfather paid his other bills by walking around town once a month carrying cash. I don't know anyone who uses this method of bill payment today. Even in my parents' generation, they put a check in an offering envelope and dropped it in the offering plate. They paid most of their bills using checks sent through the mail.

Recently I sat with my adult daughter and her husband in church. When the offering plate came, they put nothing inside and passed it right on down the line. Shocked, I expressed my surprise that they had not given to the offering. They explained that it wasn't a lack of generosity but a lack of opportunity. Neither had much cash on them that day—under $10—and both had forgotten their checkbook. As it turned out, they rarely carried cash or a checkbook. They pay for things with a credit or debit card, and they pay their bills online and have several options to do so. They then pay the credit card bill each month and avoid interest charges. When they come to church, they are motivated to give but don't have the mechanism. The church is the only place in their town that makes giving money difficult. Stores, restaurants, utilities, auto dealerships—all have multiple ways to make payments. The only place that doesn't is the church.

People in your church are more like my daughter and her husband than you may realize. True, the younger people are, the more likely they are to use electronic bill paying, but many senior citizens use them as well.

In the church I serve, about 45 percent of all donations come online. That does great things for our members. They know that no matter what is going on in their lives, whether they are on vacation or away on business, their donations are still going to the church every week. They don't miss a week and then have to remember to make it up later. As a result, they are more likely to give the amount they hoped to offer when they set their generosity goal at the beginning of the year.

Online giving also does great things for our church. Imagine if half of your income came dependably week after week after week. It would not spike way up at Easter or descend into the depths over summer vacation. As a result, the church can plan its finances with confidence.

Church leaders sometimes have objections to online giving:

It costs too much.

You have to pay about 3 percent of each donation to the service provider for online giving. I would rather not lose that 3 percent, but I know the church receives far more in contributions because of online giving. Think of how many contributions are not made when people are out of town, forget the checkbook, or didn't carry cash. Highly committed church members will often make up those donations later, but many people don't. Would you rather pay 3 percent for a dependable contribution each week, or lose 97 percent of every contribution that is not made up later? Also, keep in mind that if you tell your donors what the charge is for the online service, many will give extra to cover the cost.

It could lead to credit problems for our members.

I have heard of people getting into credit problems for many reasons: the house was too big and the mortgage too large; the car was too nice and too expensive; shopping sprees were out of control. But in all my years of ministry, I have never, ever heard of people giving in such a way as to compromise their credit. I have, however, had people thank the church for the reward points they were earning with their bank through online giving that was being paid on time and interest-free.

We don't know where to start. The easiest way to begin is to contact a third-party vendor who can assist your church. You can also ask your denomination to see what they recommend or ask a church up the street which service they use. You don't need to have the best website or a staff accountant to make this work. But you do want to pick a company that will minimize costs and provide excellent and secure service.

STEWARDSHIP THROUGHOUT THE YEAR

For the generous church, just as servanthood and the donation of time must be discussed throughout the year, financial stewardship must also be on ongoing conversation. Even after reading this far, you may find that Reluctance is telling you this can all be handled later. *Don't worry,* it whispers, *tomorrow you can figure this out. Or next week. Or in the fall when the church year really begins. Or in the winter, because fall is such a busy time....*

If you're tempted to delay, let's look at your tomorrows, or at least twelve months of them. Take out your calendar. I don't mean a metaphorical calendar; I mean open your real calendar and put some events and activities there. That calendar will guide you in the coming twelve months. Consider the following activities:

Generosity Education

Preach about stewardship for two to four weeks in the coming year. The late fall is a traditional time to talk about stewardship, encouraging people to enter a new level of discipleship including both their money and their time. Pastors who don't talk about financial stewardship doom their congregations to poor giving habits and unchallenged materialism. Put the sermon series on your calendar, and commit to casting out the demons that Reluctance has planted in your life: fear, capitulation to the stingy, and failure of prophetic nerve.

The goal of the series is to help people prayerfully consider their generosity to the church for the coming year. Many churches are not using pledge cards because of the declining rate of pledging in recent years. Reluctance loves this, because it means the church will never ask people to sit down and consider what they want to give, the same way they would consider any other expenditure, such as a house, car, or summer camp for the kids.

Every expenditure is an investment that must be considered, including the work of the church. That's why it's important to ask people annually what they want to give and request that they write it down on a card. This simple step will assist them in resizing their generosity each year as income grows or diminishes. It will also give the church an understanding of what can be accomplished in the coming year.

If you think your congregation will be hesitant to fill out "pledge cards," call them "estimate of giving cards." For some people the word *pledge* implies that if they lose a job, they won't be able to change the amount. Explain that the estimate of giving can be raised or lowered through the year with a simple call to the church office.

After you plan one sermon series, put a reminder in your calendar each quarter to talk about financial stewardship, whether in a full sermon or a sermon illustration, as a way of keeping the issue alive in the congregation.

Another good follow up to stewardship sermons is to schedule a seminar or series of classes on financial principles and practices that lead to generosity. You'll find that most people want to be generous but aren't, because they don't plan or resource their giving properly. If you help these people get serious about a budget including debt payment, saving, and spending, most of them will become generous.

Besides the important work of generosity education, your calendar can show smaller activities throughout the year that will help your church become more generous.

Seasonal Giving

To honor Christ at his birthday, you can offer an alternative giving opportunity during Advent in which the church commits its Christmas Eve offering to the poor and vulnerable. Bear in mind that a good deal of planning is required. Put related events on your calendar, then work backward to schedule conversations with your church council and finance committee so preparations can be made. Seasonal giving can be a source of great joy in a congregation when it is handled properly and celebrated.

Special Fund-raisers

Consider holding a special fund-raiser for a mission project, to offer your larger community an opportunity to be generous. Decide when the fund-raiser should be held, and adjust other fund-raising activities accordingly. In this way you can make sure your congregation does not suffer from donor fatigue, being confronted by collection after collection for a multitude of causes, such as your church, your denomination, or other local groups.

Appreciation

When planning to mail quarterly statements, consider who could write a short article describing the good things happening in your church. Work back on your calendar to contact the person and set some deadlines for their efforts.

If you plan to send a small gift and letter of appreciation at the end of the year, note when the gift will need to chosen and how you will share it with your key donors of time and money. December is a very busy month in most churches, so it's best to have this planned and ready to go by November.

THE GENEROUS CHURCH

This book began by suggesting that you consider your church brand and whether it represents values that people can trust. When considering those values, make sure to include generosity, which is at the root of everything we do to honor the teaching of Christ. When a church is true to those values and then invites its members to participate, it encourages and enables generosity.

When you communicate clearly the good news of what you accomplish, you will lift the spirit of your church members who donate their time, talent, and financial resources, and you will give them hope that their lives are important in the world. When conversations about money, possessions, and generosity become the norm for your church rather than the exception, you will move the dial on discipleship. You will help your congregation set aside the idols of our culture so they can follow the prompting of the Holy Spirit to bring good to the world.

Such churches are the ones people talk about and the ones people want to visit. It's not that you want people to glorify your church; you want them to glorify the living Christ who is at work in your church. When people visit, they will see a generous church filled with generous people who love and care for the world, who invest their time and money in ways that bring them great joy.

Years ago I was at a church leadership meeting in the rural, midsized congregation where I was pastor. Over the years our congregation had grown in its generosity and in the ministry we offered to the community. That night we had some hard decisions to make. We were considering a new ministry plan that would take time and money to accomplish. Church members would once again have to rise to the commitment of investing time and talent.

The proposal was made and accepted. Afterward, an older member named Charlotte raised her hand. "I'm not coming to these meetings anymore," she said. "They are just no fun. It used to be we would come in here and fuss and fight over the smallest of things. You couldn't spend five dollars without a debate. Now we discuss something this big, and there are people who will do it, and there is money to support it. We all just agree and go home. There is hardly a thing to argue about!"

Charlotte laughed as she shared her observation. Her humor did not mask the truth she had expressed: When resources are tight, conflict is likely; when resources are available and put to good use, people respond differently. Leadership takes on a new excitement, and people enjoy being on the same team. Charlotte didn't name it that night, but generosity had caused that change. When the church became generous, people were motivated to offer their best to God. Generosity had changed the culture of the congregation, including leadership meetings like the one she had just attended.

If I could wish anything for you, it would be that you lead in such a way that, like Charlotte and her friends, you and your friends would experience a generous church.

NOTES

1   "The Largest Auto Companies in The World 2015," *Forbes Magazine*, accessed on Feb. 9, 2015, www.forbes.com/pictures /eggh45eiki/1-toyota-motor/.

2   Jon Yeomans and Julia Bradshaw, "What happens if my VW car has emissions cheating software?," *The London Telegraph*, Nov. 4, 2015, http://www.telegraph.co.uk/finance/newsbysector/industry /11899049/What-happens-if-my-VW-car-has-emissions-cheating -software.html.

3   Mike Ramsey, "Volkswagen Emissions Problem Exposed by Routine University Research," *The Wall Street Journal*, Sep. 23, 2015, http://www.wsj.com/articles/volkswagen-emissions-problem -exposed-by-routine-university-research-1443023854.

4   Theodore Roosevelt, "Citizenship in a Republic," April 23, 1910, Paris, France, http://design.caltech.edu/erik/Misc/Citizenship_in _a_Republic.pdf.

5   Christian Smith and Hilary Davidson, *The Paradox of Generosity: Giving We Receive, Grasping We Lose* (Oxford: Oxford University Press, 2013), 102.

6   David McAllister-Wilson, "Five Guidelines for Doing Good Well," *Leading Ideas*, April 22, 2015, http://www.churchleadership.com /leadingideas/leaddocs/2015/150422_article.html.